A
BIBLE
MASTERQUIZ

D1744102

compiled by

Keith A. Mason

TRiANGlE

First published 1984
Triangle
SPCK
Holy Trinity Church
Marylebone Road
London NW1 4DU

British Library Cataloguing in Publication Data
Mason, Keith A.
  A Bible masterquiz.
  1. Bible—Examinations, questions, etc.
  I. Title
  220'.076   BS612

  ISBN 0-281-04080-X

Typeset by Pioneer, East Sussex
Printed in Great Britain by
Hazell Watson & Viney Limited,
Member of the BPCC Group,
Aylesbury, Bucks.

Introduction

This quiz book has been compiled with great care. Much consideration has been given to the quality of the questions, that they should be suitable for both well-established Christians and beginners.

The Authorized King James Version of the Bible has been used as a source of reference, and the relevant text has been quoted with each answer. This should prove useful in the case of a query, or if the book is being used as a source of information for study groups.

The answers to each page of questions are printed on the reverse page, which allows the question-master to skip from question to answer and back again without much trouble, thus eliminating the old problem of having to keep one finger in the question page while using the other hand to look up the relevant answer at the back of the book; a practice which often resulted in both pages being lost, creating chaos.

This book is ideal for people of all ages, with the exception of the very young, but certainly Sunday school groups, youth groups, fellowship groups, and main congregational bodies should find its contents to be of interest as well as having the ability to make them think, which is surely the aim of any quiz.

1. Who said: 'Woe is me! for I am undone; because I am a man of unclean lips, and I dwell in the midst of a people of unclean lips: for mine eyes have seen the King, the Lord of hosts.'?

2. In which city was Jesus born?

3. In which province was Bethlehem situated?

4. Whose diet consisted of locusts and wild honey?

5. Who was thrown into a lion's den because he would not stop praying to the one true God?

6. Who climbed into a sycamore tree to get a better view of Jesus, because he was too small to see over the crowd of people?

7. In which city did the event of the previous question take place?

8. Who was Jacob's brother?

9. Who was given a coat of many colours by his father?

10. What is the eighth commandment?

11. Who was turned into a pillar of salt?

12. How much did Jesus say that two sparrows were sold for?

13. Which two Gospel writers were not included in the original twelve disciples?

1. *Isaiah. Isa. 6.5.*

2. *Bethlehem. Matt. 2.1.*

3. *Judaea. Matt. 2.1.*

4. *John the Baptist. Matt. 3.4.*

5. *Daniel. Dan. 6.16.*

6. *Zacchaeus. Luke 19.2-4.*

7. *Jericho. Luke 19.1.*

8. *Esau. Gen. 25.26.*

9. *Joseph. Gen. 37.3.*

10. *'Thou shalt not steal.' Exod. 20.15.*

11. *Lot's wife. Gen. 19.26.*

12. *A farthing. Matt. 10.29.*

13. *Luke and Mark. Matt. 10.1-4.*

14. How tall was Goliath?

15. Upon which mountains did Noah's ark come to rest after the flood?

16. How long did the flood waters remain upon the earth?

17. What was the name of Samuel's mother?

18. Who were the first two disciples of Jesus?

19. Who is the oldest man in the Bible, and how long did he live?

20. When the ark of the covenant was being moved to a different place by King David, the oxen which were pulling the cart stumbled, and somebody reached out and touched the ark to help him keep his balance and was struck dead. Who was it?

21. Who was just about to sacrifice his own son, but was stopped by the voice of an angel?

22. How many psalms are there in the book of Psalms?

23. Which kind of wood was Noah told to use in the building of the ark?

24. What was the name of Moses' son?

25. What were the names of the three men who were cast into a fiery furnace because they would not bow down to, nor worship, a golden image, yet came out of the furnace unharmed?

3

14. *Six cubits and a span. (About eleven feet and a half.) 1 Sam. 17.4.*

15. *Ararat. Gen. 8.4.*

16. *One hundred and fifty days. Gen. 7.24.*

17. *Hannah. 1 Sam. 1.20.*

18. *Simon Peter and Andrew. Matt. 4.18.*

19. *Methuselah, nine hundred and sixty nine years. Gen. 5.27.*

20. *Uzzah. 2 Sam. 6.6-7.*

21. *Abraham. Gen. 22.10-11.*

22. *150.*

23. *Gopher wood. Gen. 6.14.*

24. *Gershom. Exod. 2.22.*

25. *Shadrach, Meshach and Abednego. Dan. 3.20.*

26. After Jesus had been baptized, he went into the wilderness to be tempted of the devil, where he prayed and fasted. How long did he remain there?

27. In which city was Jesus brought up?

28. Which mountain was Moses upon when he saw the burning bush?

29. What was the name of the Pharisee who came to Jesus by night, and was told that a man must be born again?

30. How many of each kind of animal was Noah told to take into the ark?

31. Which king saw fingers of a hand write the words 'MENE, MENE, TEKEL, UPHARSIN' upon the wall of the palace, and was greatly troubled by the incident?

32. How many plagues were sent upon Egypt?

33. Who was saved from being killed, by his mother hiding him in an ark made of bulrushes, slime and pitch?

34. Who was cured of his leprosy by washing himself in Jordan seven times?

35. How many pieces of silver were paid to Judas Iscariot in payment for betraying Jesus?

36. According to Genesis, on which day was man created?

26. *Forty days and forty nights. Matt. 4.2.*

27. *Nazareth. Matt 2.23.*

28. *Horeb. Exod. 3.1-3.*

29. *Nicodemus. John 3.1-3.*

30. *Seven of each kind of clean animals, and two of each kind of unclean animals. Gen. 7.2.*

31. *Belshazzar. Dan. 5.1-6, 25.*

32. *Ten. Exod. chs. 7—11.*

33. *Moses. Exod. 2.3.*

34. *Naaman. 2 Kings 5.*

35. *Thirty. Matt. 26.15.*

36. *The sixth day. Gen. 1.26-31.*

37. In which city are we told that the disciples were first called Christians?

38. What was torn into two halves at the moment of Jesus' death?

39. Which river did John the Baptist use to baptize people in?

40. After Jesus' birth, Joseph was warned in a dream to take his wife and child, and to flee for safety from King Herod. Where was he told to flee to?

41. What age group of children did King Herod order to be killed in an attempt to destroy Jesus?

42. Who was Abraham's wife?

43. In the life of Jesus, a centurion was commended for his faith because he believed that Jesus could cure his servant simply by command without even visiting the sick man. What was the servant suffering from?

44. Who wrote the book 'The Acts of the Apostles'?

45. To whom was it written?

46. How many people were saved from the flood in the ark?

47. Which mountain did Moses ascend to receive the ten commandments?

37. *Antioch. Acts 11.26.*

38. *The veil of the temple. Mark 15.38.*

39. *Jordan. Matt. 3.6.*

40. *Egypt. Matt. 2.13.*

41. *Two years old and under. Matt. 2.16.*

42. *Sarai. Gen. 11.29. Later called Sarah (Gen. 17.15).*

43. *Palsy. Matt. 8.6.*

44. *Luke.*

45. *Theophilus. Acts 1.1.*

46. *Eight. 1 Pet. 3.20.*

47. *Sinai. Exod. 19.20.*

48. Who was Isaac's wife?

49. Which Old Testament prophet foretold the coming of John the Baptist and the message that he would preach?

50. What is the interpretation of the word Emmanuel?

51. How many days was Jonah in the belly of the fish?

52. Which of the twelve disciples was arrested with Peter, after a lame man had been healed?

53. Which psalm begins with the words: 'He that dwelleth in the secret place of the most High shall abide under the shadow of the Almighty'?

54. What is the more common name by which the sea of Tiberias is better known?

55. Habakkuk, the prophet, wrote the words '. . . the just shall live by his faith.' How many times are these words quoted in the New Testament?

56. Which one of the disciples would not believe that Jesus had risen from the dead until he had actually seen him, complete with nail prints?

57. Who was compelled to carry Jesus' cross to the place of execution?

58. Of which people was Goliath the champion fighter?

48. *Rebekah. Gen. 24.67.*

49. *Isaiah. Matt. 3.3.*

50. *God with us. Matt. 1.23.*

51. *Three days and three nights. Jonah 1.17.*

52. *John. Acts 4.13-14.*

53. *Psalm 91.*

54. *The sea of Galilee. John 6.1.*

55. *Three times. Rom. 1.17. Gal. 3.11. Heb. 10.38*

56. *Thomas. John 20.24-28.*

57. *Simon of Cyrene. Matt. 27.32.*

58. *The Philistines. 1 Sam. 17.4.*

59. What was the name of the felon who was released from the death penalty in place of Jesus, according to the will of the people?

60. Who was Moses' wife?

61. Which one of the disciples drew his sword, and cut off the high priest's servant's right ear, in an attempt to prevent the capture of Jesus?

62. What was Jesus' first miracle?

63. How many jars of water did Jesus change into wine?

64. How many disciples were present with Jesus on the mountain when he was transfigured?

65. Who were they?

66. Who else did they see on the mountain, talking with Jesus?

67. Which of the disciples denied Jesus three times as Jesus had prophesied that he would?

68. Who was the first person to ask Peter if he knew Jesus?

69. The third person to ask Peter the question had a strange, significant connection with him, what was it?

70. What colour was the robe that Pilate clothed Jesus in, to mock him?

59. *Barabbas. Luke 23.18.*

60. *Zipporah. Exod. 2.21.*

61. *Simon Peter. John 18.10.*

62. *The changing of water into wine. John 2.1-11.*

63. *Six. John 2.6.*

64. *Three. Matt. 17.1.*

65. *Peter, James and John. Matt. 17.1.*

66. *Moses and Elias, (Elijah). Matt. 17.3.*

67. *Peter. Matt. 26.75.*

68. *The damsel that kept the door of the high priest's palace. John 18.17.*

69. *He was the kinsman of the man whose ear Peter had cut off. John 18.26.*

70. *Purple. John 19.2.*

71. To which of the disciples did Jesus pass on the responsibility of looking after Mary, his mother?

72. What was the superscription which was written above Jesus' head on the cross, by Pilate?

73. In how many different languages was the superscription written, and what were they?

74. To which group of people was Diana the goddess?

75. What were the two foods that God sent the Children of Israel when they were in the wilderness?

76. How many pieces of silver was Joseph sold by his brethren for?

77. How many times did Jesus tell us that we must forgive our enemies?

78. Who was Moses' sister?

79. Where did God tell Jonah to go to, and call the people to repent?

80. What was Jesus given to drink when he spoke the words 'I thirst'?

81. What was the name of Jesus' follower who begged Pilate for the body of Jesus, and laid it in the sepulchre?

71. *John. John 19.26-27.*

72. *This is the King of the Jews. Luke 23.38.*

73. *Three. Greek, Latin and Hebrew. Luke 23.38.*

74. *The Ephesians. Acts 19.34, 35.*

75. *Quails and manna. Exod. 16.*

76. *Twenty. Gen. 37.28.*

77. *Seventy times seven. Matt. 18.22.*

78. *Miriam. Num. 26.59.*

79. *Nineveh. Jonah 1.2.*

80. *Vinegar. John 19.29.*

81. *Joseph of Arimathaea. John 19.38-42.*

82. Who brought a hundred pounds weight of myrrh and aloes for Jesus' body?

83. What was the name of the place where Jesus was crucified, and what is its interpretation?

84. What position of authority did Pontius Pilate hold?

85. What was the name of the pool by which numerous people gathered to be cured of their diseases, by getting into the water first after the water had been moved by an angel?

86. Which famous chapter begins with the words: 'Let not your heart be troubled: ye believe in God, believe also in me.'?

87. Where was Jesus when Judas Iscariot came with the Jewish leaders to betray him?

88. In order to get from the city to the garden a brook had to be crossed, what was it called?

89. How many sons did Jacob have?

90. Name them.

91. Who preached to a eunuch while travelling in a chariot?

92. What nationality was the eunuch?

93. Who contracted leprosy for speaking out against Moses?

82. *Nicodemus. John 19.39.*

83. *Golgotha, The place of a skull. Mark 15.22.*

84. *Governor. Matt. 27.2.*

85. *Bethesda. John 5.2.*

86. *John 14.*

87. *Gethsemane. Matt. 26.36.*

88. *Cedron. John 18.1.*

89. *Twelve. Gen. 35.22.*

90. *Reuben, Simeon, Levi, Judah, Issachar, Zebulun, Dan, Naphtali, Gad, Asher, Joseph, Benjamin.*

91. *Philip. Acts 8.26-39.*

92. *Ethiopian. Acts 8.27.*

93. *Miriam. Num. 12.*

94. In the miracle of the feeding of the five thousand, how many loaves and how many fishes were used?

95. After the same miracle, how many baskets of fragments were gathered up?

96. A second, similar miracle was also performed by Jesus a short while after. How many were fed on this second occasion?

97. When in contention with the Pharisees, John the Baptist declared that God was able to raise up children to Abraham from certain things, what were they?

98. Whom did Jesus command to 'Come forth' from the tomb, after he had been dead for four days?

99. How many sisters did Lazarus have, and what were their names?

100. What is the shortest verse in the Bible?

101. What is it that is said to be more precious than rubies (or jewels)?

102. What was the object that was placed in the mouth of Benjamin's sack of corn by Joseph's steward?

103. Which Psalm is split into twenty-two sections, each one being marked by a letter of the Hebrew alphabet?

94. *Five loaves and two fishes. John 6.9.*

95. *Twelve. John 6.13.*

96. *Four thousand men, besides women and children. Matt. 15.38.*

97. *Stones. Matt. 3.9.*

98. *Lazarus. John 11.43.*

99. *Two, Mary and Martha. John 11.1.*

100. *'Jesus wept.' John 11.35.*

101. *Wisdom. Prov. 3.13-15 or A good woman (Prov. 31.10).*

102. *Joseph's silver cup. Gen. 44.2.*

103. *Psalm 119.*

104. On which isle was the disciple John when he wrote the book of Revelation?

105. Which disciple walked on the water towards Jesus?

106. Which of the original twelve disciples was a publican?

107. What was a publican?

108. Whose rod budded, bloomed blossoms, and yielded almonds?

109. What was the name of the street into which Ananias was told to go in search of Saul?

110. What was the apostle Paul's name before it was changed?

111. From which city did he originate?

112. Who was Joshua's father?

113. Who said: 'I have heard of thee by the hearing of the ear: but now mine eye seeth thee. Wherefore I abhor myself, and repent in dust and ashes.'?

114. What relation was Ruth to Naomi?

115. Ruth was not a Jewess; from which people did she originate?

116. What is the sixth commandment?

104. *Patmos. Rev. 1.9.*

105. *Peter. Matt. 14.29.*

106. *Matthew. Matt. 9.9.*

107. *A tax gatherer.*

108. *Aaron's. Num. 17.8.*

109. *Straight. Acts 9.11.*

110. *Saul. Acts 13.9.*

111. *Tarsus. Acts 21.39.*

112. *Nun. Josh. 1.1.*

113. *Job. Job 42.5-6.*

114. *Daughter-in-law. Ruth 1.22.*

115. *The Moabites. Ruth 1.4.*

116. *Thou shalt not kill. Exod. 20.13.*

117. What was the name of the priest into whose care the young child Samuel was placed?

118. What were the names of Eli's two sons?

119. Who sold his birthright for a meal of pottage?

120. What was the token that God gave Noah as a perpetual reminder that He would never flood the earth again?

121. What were the names of Noah's three sons?

122. In the book of Genesis we are given an account of how men planned to build a tower. What was it called, and in which land was it situated?

123. Which city developed in the same place as the tower, and is often used as an example by God as a representative of evil?

124. What relation was Abraham to Lot?

125. Why did Abraham and Lot part company?

126. Which two cities did God destroy with fire and brimstone?

127. At which hour was Jesus crucified?

128. At which hour did Jesus die?

117. *Eli. 1 Sam. 3.1.*

118. *Hophni and Phinehas. 1 Sam. 1.3.*

119. *Esau. Gen. 25.29-34.*

120. *The rainbow. Gen. 9.11-16.*

121. *Shem, Ham and Japheth. Gen. 10.1.*

122. *The tower of Babel, in the land of Shinar. Gen. 11.1-9.*

123. *Babylon.*

124. *Uncle. Gen. 14.12.*

125. *There was strife between their herdmen. Gen. 13.7-8.*

126. *Sodom and Gomorrah. Gen. 19.24.*

127. *The third hour. Mark 15.25.*

128. *The ninth hour. Mark 15.34.*

129. Out of the six hours that Jesus was on the cross, for how many hours did darkness cover the land?

130. What were the centurion's words immediately after Jesus' death?

131. What was the name of the coppersmith of whom Paul complained because he had done him much evil?

132. How many books are there in the Old Testament?

133. How many books are there in the New Testament?

134. One of the rulers of the synagogue had a daughter who was brought back to life by Jesus. What was his name?

135. How old was his daughter?

136. While Jesus was travelling to Jairus' house a woman was cured from an issue of blood. How was the cure implemented?

137. How long had the woman been suffering from her illness?

138. Before Isaac was born, Abraham had a child by his wife's handmaid. What was her name?

139. What was the name of the child?

129. *Three. Mark 15.33.*

130. *'Truly this man was the Son of God.'*
     Mark 15.39.

131. *Alexander. 2 Tim. 4.14.*

132. *39.*

133. *27.*

134. *Jairus. Mark 5.22.*

135. *About twelve years old. Luke 8.42.*

136. *She touched the border of his garment.*
     Luke 8.44.

137. *Twelve years. Luke 8.43.*

138. *Hagar. Gen. 16.15.*

139. *Ishmael. Gen. 16.15.*

140. How many angels appeared to Abraham whilst journeying to Sodom to destroy it?

141. What was Sarah's reaction when she was told by one of the visitors that she would have a child?

142. After talking with Abraham, the Lord said that he would not destroy Sodom if he found a certain minimum number of righteous souls there. How many?

143. How old was Abraham when Isaac was born?

144. How were the wise men guided to the place where Jesus was born?

145. What was the food and drink that Daniel asked for in preference to the king's meat and wine?

146. For what purpose had King Nebuchadnezzar taken Daniel and his companions into the palace in the first place?

147. Who set the Philistines' corn on fire by tying firebrands on to foxes' tails and letting them loose?

148. How did the Philistines retaliate?

149. Which city did the disciples Philip, Peter and Andrew come from?

140. *Three. Gen. 18.2.*

141. *She laughed. Gen. 18.12.*

142. *Ten. Gen. 18.32.*

143. *A hundred years old. Gen. 21.5.*

144. *By a star. Matt. 2.9.*

145. *Pulse and water. Dan. 1.12.*

146. *Because they were skilful in all wisdom, cunning in knowledge, and understanding science. Dan. 1.4.*

147. *Samson. Judg. 15.4-5.*

148. *They burned Samson's ex-wife and his father-in-law. Judg. 15.6.*

149. *Bethsaida. John 1.44.*

150. After Philip had been called to be a disciple, he went to fetch Nathanael, telling him that he had 'found Him, of whom Moses in the law, and the prophets, did write, Jesus of Nazareth.' What was Nathanael's reply?

151. Where was the wedding feast being held when Jesus turned the water into wine?

152. Which queen came to Jerusalem to prove Solomon with hard questions, because she had heard of his great wisdom concerning the things of God?

153. A prophet went to Bethel to prophesy against King Jeroboam and was later torn by a lion because he disobeyed God by staying in the vicinity for a meal. What was the name of the child he said would be born to the house of David?

154. After the death of Sarah, Abraham remarried. What was his new wife's name?

155. How old was Abraham when he died?

156. What relation was Laban to Jacob?

157. What was Esau out hunting for when Jacob deceived his father and stole Esau's blessing?

158. Who dreamed a dream in which the sun, the moon and the eleven stars made obeisance to him?

150. *'Can there any good thing come out of Nazareth?' John 1.46.*

151. *Cana of Galilee. John 2.11.*

152. *The queen of Sheba. 1 Kings 10.1.*

153. *Josiah. 1 Kings 13.1-4.*

154. *Keturah. Gen. 25.1.*

155. *175 years. Gen. 25.7.*

156. *His uncle. Gen. 27.43.*

157. *Venison. Gen. 27.3.*

158. *Joseph. Gen. 37.9.*

159. Which land inside Egypt was given to Jacob and his sons by Pharaoh, so that they would have somewhere safe to live during the great famine?

160. How many sons did Joseph have?

161. What were their names?

162. What gifts did the wise men bring from the east to the baby Jesus?

163. Matthew quotes a prophecy of Jeremiah, the prophet, in this way: 'In Rama there was a voice heard, lamentation, and weeping, and great mourning, Rachel weeping for her children, and would not be comforted, because they are not.' How did Matthew say this had been fulfilled?

164. When Herod died, his son took his place, what was his name?

165. Finish the following text: 'For to him that is joined to all the living there is hope: for . . .'

166. What special gift did God give Daniel?

167. King Nebuchadnezzar dreamed a dream, and he called for his magicians, astrologers and sorcerers to interpret it. What were the king's conditions to ensure that the magicians were telling him the truth, and not just making it all up?

168. Which kingdom did Nebuchadnezzar rule over?

159. *Goshen. Gen. 47.6.*

160. *Two. Gen. 48.1.*

161. *Ephraim and Manasseh. Gen. 48.1.*

162. *Gold, frankincense and myrrh. Matt. 2.11.*

163. *By the slaughter of the children carried out by Herod, in an attempt to kill the baby Jesus. Matt. 2.16-18.*

164. *Archelaus. Matt. 2.22.*

165. *'. . . a living dog is better than a dead lion.' Eccles. 9.4.*

166. *Understanding of dreams and visions. Dan. 1.17.*

167. *They not only had to tell the king the interpretation, but the dream also. Dan. 2.9.*

168. *Babylon. Dan. 1.1.*

169. After Aaron's death who took his place?

170. What was his name?

171. Who was confronted with a talking ass?

172. How many angels appeared to the disciples after Jesus had ascended into the cloud, to tell them that He would return in a like manner?

173. From which mountain did Jesus ascend into heaven after He had risen from the dead?

174. What was the name of the field which was purchased with the thirty pieces of silver that Judas received from the Pharisees for betraying Jesus?

175. What is the interpretation of the word — Aceldama?

176. In Acts chapter 12, which of the original twelve disciples did Herod kill?

177. What was it that Jesus told us to consider, how they toil not, neither do they spin, yet Solomon in all his glory was not arrayed like one of them?

178. To whom was the gospel of St Luke written?

179. What is it that is 'sufficient unto the day'?

169. *His son. Num. 20.26.*

170. *Eleazar. Num. 20.25.*

171. *Balaam. Num. 22.30.*

172. *Two. Acts 1.10.*

173. *Olivet. Acts 1.12.*

174. *Aceldama. Acts 1.19.*

175. *The field of blood. Acts 1.19.*

176. *James the brother of John. Acts 12.2.*

177. *The lilies of the field. Matt. 6.28-29.*

178. *Theophilus. Luke 1.3.*

179. *'The evil thereof.' Matt. 6.34.*

180. What was the name of the angel who was sent to Mary to tell her about the conception and birth of Jesus?

181. What did Jesus say would happen if the blind led the blind?

182. Was Simon Peter married or single?

183. What were the names of two magicians of Egypt who turned their rods into serpents in answer to Moses' and Aaron's miracle?

184. What is the ninth commandment?

185. Finish the following text: 'Blessed are the pure in heart . . .'

186. What was the name of Moses' father-in-law, who was also the priest of Midian?

187. How old was Moses when he returned to Egypt and asked Pharaoh for the release of the Hebrews?

188. What was the first miracle that Aaron performed before Pharaoh?

189. How did God lead the children of Israel through the wilderness, so that they could travel both by day and by night?

190. How old was Jesus when Mary and Joseph took him up to Jerusalem and lost him?

180. *Gabriel. Luke 1.26.*

181. *They would both fall into the ditch. Matt. 15.14.*

182. *Married. Matt. 8.14.*

183. *Jannes and Jambres. 2 Tim. 3.8.*

184. *'Thou shalt not bear false witness against thy neighbour.' Exod. 20.16.*

185. *'. . . for they shall see God.' Matt. 5.8.*

186. *Jethro. Exod. 3.1.*

187. *Eighty. Exod. 7.7.*

188. *His rod was turned into a serpent. Exod. 7.10.*

189. *A pillar of cloud went before them by day, and a pillar of fire by night. Exod. 13.21.*

190. *Twelve. Luke 2.42.*

191. Why did they go up to Jerusalem in the first place?

192. How many days passed before they found Jesus again?

193. After they had found him in the temple asking the teachers questions, they rebuked him for acting as he had done. How did Jesus reply to their rebuke?

194. How many men is Samson reputed to have killed with the jawbone of an ass?

195. What was the name of the woman whom Samson loved after the death of his first wife, who also betrayed him?

196. Who was Methuselah's father?

197. How did God punish Nebuchadnezzar because he was so proud, and unmerciful towards the poor?

198. What was so special about a decree that had been made according to the Medes and Persians by a king?

199. What happened to those men who had accused Daniel to the king, causing him to be thrown into the den of lions?

200. Which prophet was fed by ravens while the country he was in was in a state of drought and famine?

191. *To celebrate the feast of the passover. Luke 2.41.*

192. *Three. Luke 2.46.*

193. *'How is it that ye sought me? Wist ye not that I must be about my Father's business?' Luke 2.49.*

194. *A thousand. Judg. 15.15.*

195. *Delilah. Judg. 16.4.*

196. *Enoch. Genesis 5.21 and Luke 3.37.*

197. *For seven years he became mad, eating grass like an animal. Dan. 4.33.*

198. *Once given it could not be repealed. Dan. 6.12.*

199. *They were thrown in themselves. Dan. 6.24.*

200. *Elijah. 1 Kings 17.1-6.*

201. From which people did Elijah originate?

202. Elijah had great trouble with the prophets of Baal, who kept on leading the people away from God to the worship of idols. So he put them to a test to find out which of them worshipped the true God, what was it?

203. How many prophets of Baal were there?

204. How long did Baal's prophets cry to him to send fire?

205. Elijah's prayers were answered and God sent fire from heaven to burn the sacrifice, but how did Elijah deliberately make the miracle even more outstanding?

206. After the death of Judas Iscariot the other disciples decided that their number should be renewed to twelve and two names were nominated to be voted on; who were they?

207. Who won the vote?

208. Who said: 'Silver and gold have I none; but such as I have give I thee: In the name of Jesus Christ of Nazareth rise up and walk.'?

209. What were the names of the man and wife who sold a possession, but kept back part of the price, for which cheating they both died according to the prophecy of Peter?

210. What was the possession that they sold?

201. *He was a Tishbite from Gilead.*
     1 Kings 17.1.

202. *Both he and Baal's prophets would build an altar, complete with sacrifice, and they would each pray to their God to send down fire from heaven to set it alight. 1 Kings 18.23-24.*

203. *450. 1 Kings 18.19.*

204. *From morning until evening. 1 Kings 18.26-9.*

205. *He poured twelve barrels of water over the altar beforehand. 1 Kings 18.33, 34.*

206. *Joseph Justus and Matthias. Acts 1.23.*

207. *Matthias. Acts 1.26.*

208. *Peter. Acts 3.6.*

209. *Ananias and Sapphira. Acts 5.1-10.*

210. *Some land. Acts 5.3.*

211. What was the name of the young man who, after giving a good defence as witness to the Jews concerning Jesus, was cast out of the city and stoned to death?

212. How many years did the Jews tell Jesus that it had taken to build the temple at Jerusalem?

213. The people who witnessed the stoning of Stephen laid their clothes down at the feet of a man who was then consenting to the action, but was later to become the prime teacher of the gospel; who was he?

214. What were Stephen's last words?

215. What was the name of the sorcerer in Samaria, who offered Peter money in exchange for the power to do miracles?

216. After Saul had been converted, he preached the gospel in Damascus, the very city where he had gone with the intention of putting down the Christian uprising. The Jews were so angry with Saul for changing sides that they put a guard on all of the city's gates, plotting to kill him. How did he escape?

217. What nationality was the woman at Jacob's well, of whom Jesus first asked a drink, then offered to give her 'living water'?

218. Why did this act of Jesus' seem so odd to the woman, so much so, that she questioned his action?

211. *Stephen. Acts 7.59.*

212. *46 years. John 2.20.*

213. *Saul, later called Paul. Acts 7.58.*

214. *'Lord, lay not this sin to their charge.'*
     Acts 7.60.

215. *Simon. Acts 8.9.*

216. *The other disciples took him by night and*
     lowered him over the city wall in a basket.
     Acts 9.25.

217. *A Samaritan. John 4.7.*

218. *The Jews had no dealings with the*
     Samaritans. John 4.9.

219. Jesus healed a crippled man who was lying at the pool of Bethesda, who told Jesus that somebody else always got into the water before him after the angel had troubled it. How long had this man had his infirmity?

220. When the Pharisees were all plotting against Jesus, which one of them stood up for him, saying the words: 'Doth our law judge any man, before it hear him, and know what he doeth?'

221. A woman was brought to Jesus by the Pharisees accused of adultery, which was an offence punishable by death by stoning. How did Jesus answer them?

222. After King Herod had killed James the brother of John, he took Peter also, and threw him into prison. How many soldiers did he order to guard Peter?

223. How did Peter escape?

224. What did Herod do to the keepers of the prison?

225. Who was it that brought a box of very precious ointment, and anointed the feet of Jesus with it?

226. Her action caused some indignation among others who were present, because they thought it was a great waste to use such precious ointment in this way. How much was it said to be worth?

219.   *Thirty-eight years. John 5.5.*

220.   *Nicodemus. John 7.51.*

221.   *'He that is without sin among you, let him first cast a stone at her.' John 8.7.*

222.   *Four quaternions, (16 men). Acts 12.4.*

223.   *An angel freed him from his chains and guided him to the outside of the prison. Acts 12.7-10.*

224.   *Condemned them to death. Acts 12.19.*

225.   *Mary, the sister of Lazarus. John 12.3.*

226.   *Three hundred pence. Mark 14.5.*

227. In one of Jesus' miracles he made clay with spittle, and anointed the eyes of a blind man, then told him to go and wash himself in a certain pool; which pool was it?

228. In the opening chapters of the book of Revelation there are certain messages to the churches, how many churches are there?

229. What was it that Jesus said was '. . . good for nothing, but to be cast out, and to be trodden under foot of men.'?

230. In which of the four gospels is *The Lord's Prayer* recorded?

231. After three days journeying in the wilderness of Shur the Hebrews came to a place where there was water, but it was undrinkable because of its bitter taste. What was the place called?

232. What did Moses do to make the water sweet enough to drink?

233. Who said: 'Is not this great Babylon, that I have built for the house of the kingdom by the might of my power, and for the honour of my majesty.'?

234. After Peter's miraculous escape from prison, to which house did he go?

235. What was the name of the damsel who answered the door to Peter's knocking, then left him standing outside in her excitement while she ran to tell the others?

227. *The pool of Siloam. John 9.7.*

228. *Seven. Rev. 1.11.*

229. *Salt that had lost its savour.*
     Matt. 5.13.

230. *Matthew and Luke. Matt. 6.9-13;*
     Luke 11.2-4.

231. *Marah. Exod. 15.23.*

232. *He threw a tree into the water. Exod. 15.25.*

233. *Nebuchadnezzar. Dan. 4.30*

234. *The house of Mary, the mother of John Mark.*
     Acts 12.12.

235. *Rhoda. Acts 12.13.*

236. When Saul and Barnabas went to Paphos, a false prophet and sorcerer withstood them, what was his name?

237. What was the result of Bar-jesus' attempts to turn the people away from the gospel that Saul was teaching?

238. Why was Moses not allowed to enter into The Promised Land?

239. Who was appointed to take charge of the remainder of the journey in Moses' place?

240. Which mountain did Moses ascend to look over the promised land which he could never enter?

241. Finish the following text: 'Come unto me, all ye that labour and are heavy laden . . .'

242. At Joppa there was a certain disciple who had made many coats and clothes for the poor, but she had died, and her friends sent for Peter. What was her name?

243. What did Peter do?

244. While Peter was at Joppa he resided with a tanner called Simon, and one day while on the roof of Simon's house he saw a vision of a great sheet let down from heaven. What was in the sheet?

236. *Bar-jesus or Elymas. Acts 13.6-8.*

237. *He was made blind for a season.*
Acts 13.10-11.

238. *Because he rebelled against God's*
commandment and struck the rock twice in
the desert of Zin. Num. 27.13-14.

239. *Joshua. Num. 27.18-20.*

240. *Mount Nebo. Deut. 32.49.*

241. *'. . . and I will give you rest.' Matt. 11.28.*

242. *Tabitha, or Dorcas. Acts 9.36.*

243. *He turned all of the mourners out of the*
room, kneeled down, prayed, and said the
words; 'Tabitha, arise,' at which she opened
her eyes and sat up. Acts 9.40.

244. *All manner of four-footed beasts, wild beasts,*
creeping things, and fowls of the air. Acts
10.11-12.

245. A voice in the vision said: 'Rise, Peter; kill, and eat.' Peter answered, 'Not so, Lord; for I have never eaten any thing that is common or unclean.' What was the answer that God gave to Peter?

246. How many times was this same vision shown to Peter?

247. Paul and Barnabas went to Lycaonia, where they preached the gospel and were received with such enthusiasm that somebody was going to perform a sacrifice before the people in their honour. Who was he?

248. The same people believed that Paul and Barnabas were gods, and they gave them names according to their status. What did they call Barnabas?

249. What did they call Paul?

250. What was the name of the sea which God parted, opening a path through the middle for the Children of Israel to pass through?

251. What is the fifth commandment?

252. After Jesus' resurrection from the dead, several disciples went out fishing all night and they caught nothing. In the morning Jesus appeared on the shore and told them to do something, what was it?

253. How many fish did they catch as a result?

245. *'What God hath cleansed, that call not thou common.' Acts 10.15.*

246. *Three times. Acts 10.16.*

247. *The priest of Jupiter. Acts 14.13.*

248. *Jupiter. Acts 14.12.*

249. *Mercurius. Acts 14.12.*

250. *The Red sea. Exod. 13.18.*

251. *'Honour thy father and thy mother.' Exod. 20.12.*

252. *He told them to cast their net on the right side of the ship. John 21.6.*

253. *153 large fish. John 21.11.*

254. After the fish breakfast Jesus asked Peter the same question three times. What was it?

255. Finish the following text: 'He hath showed thee, O man, what is good; and what doth the Lord require of thee . . .'

256. To which church does God say, 'I know thy works, that thou art neither cold nor hot: I would thou wert cold or hot. So then because thou art luke-warm, and neither cold nor hot, I will spue thee out of my mouth.'?

257. How many other men were crucified along with Jesus?

258. While Paul and Barnabas were at Lystra, certain Jews came from Antioch and turned the people against both them and their gospel teaching. What happened to Paul as a result?

259. Why did they leave off stoning him before he was dead?

260. What nationality was Timothy's father?

261. What was the name of the woman from the city of Thyatira, who was a seller of purple, and insisted that Paul and Silas should lodge with her?

262. How did Elijah die?

263. What did Elisha cry out when he saw Elijah taken up?

254. *'Lovest thou me?' John 21.15-17.*

255. *'. . . but to do justly, and to love mercy, and to walk humbly with thy God.' Micah 6.8.*

256. *The church of the Laodiceans. Rev. 3.14-16.*

257. *Two. Mark 15.27.*

258. *They stoned him. Acts 14.19.*

259. *They thought that he was dead, but he revived. Acts 14.19-20.*

260. *A Greek. Acts 16.1.*

261. *Lydia. Acts 16.14-15.*

262. *He was taken up to heaven in a whirlwind. 2 Kings 2.11.*

263. *'My father, my father, the chariot of Israel, and the horsemen thereof.' 2 Kings 2.12.*

264. Of which animal did the children of Israel make themselves a golden image to worship, while Moses wasn't there?

265. Where was Moses at the time?

266. When Moses came back down his frustration and anger were so great that he smashed the tablets of stone on which the commandments were written. What did he do with the golden calf?

267. The Nazarites were a sect who had vowed a vow of separation unto God. Their vow contained such things as abstaining from all wine, strong drink, vinegar, fruits of the vine, etc., but there was something else much more well known, what was it?

268. Who was the famous Nazarite who was lulled into breaking his vow, with disastrous results?

269. What is the theme of the thirteenth chapter of first Corinthians?

270. What mixture was offered to Jesus as a pain reliever before he was crucified, but he refused it?

271. What was the disciple Thomas' other name?

272. In which wilderness did John the Baptist begin to preach his message of repentance?

273. What relation was John the Baptist to Jesus?

264. *A calf. Exod. 32.4.*

265. *At the top of mount Sinai. Exod. 31.18 — 32.1.*

266. *He burnt it, ground it to powder, mixed it with water and made the children of Israel drink it. Exod. 32.20.*

267. *They had to let their hair grow. Num. 6.5.*

268. *Samson. Judg. 16.19.*

269. *Charity, or Love.*

270. *Wine mingled with myrrh. Mark 15.23.*

271. *Didymus, or The Twin. John 21.2.*

272. *Judaea. Matt. 3.1.*

273. *Jesus' mother was John's mother's cousin. Luke 1.36.*

274. What thing did David and his men eat in the house of God, something which ought not to have been eaten by anybody except the priests?

275. Finish the following text: 'Judge not . . .'

276. After Elijah had been taken up in the whirlwind, how many of the sons of the prophets went in search in case God had set him down on a mountain somewhere?

277. What article of clothing did Elijah leave behind for Elisha?

278. What was it about the sons of Anak that caused the children of Israel to fear them so much?

279. What is Korah remembered for most?

280. Which New Testament writer likens those who oppose the gospel to Korah?

281. What was the recognized amount that the Jews had to pay to their priests in tithe?

282. How many times did Moses strike the rock to bring forth water, while they were in the desert of Zin?

283. Why did God take Aaron's life from him, and not allow him to enter into The Promised Land?

284. Name the seven churches in the first three chapters of Revelation that John was told to write to.

274. *The shewbread. Luke 6.3-4.*

275. *'. . . that ye be not judged.' Matt. 7.1.*

276. *Fifty. 2 Kings 2.16.*

277. *His mantle. 2 Kings 2.13.*

278. *They were giants. Num. 13.33.*

279. *His rebellion against Moses and Aaron. Num. 16.*

280. *Jude. Jude 11.*

281. *A tenth of their income. Num. 18.*

282. *Twice. Num. 20.11.*

283. *Because he and Moses had rebelled against God's word at the water of Meribah. Num. 20. 24.*

284. *Ephesus, Smyrna, Pergamos, Thyatira, Sardis, Philadelphia, and Laodicea. Rev. chs. 2 and 3.*

285. Who was the father of James and John?

286. In which epistle does the writer elaborate upon the mysterious high priest called Melchisedec?

287. Complete the following text: 'It is easier for a camel to go through a needle's eye . . .'

288. What good advice does Paul give to 'him that thinketh he standeth . . .'?

289. To which church did Paul write, calling them foolish, and asking them who had bewitched them?

290. According to the prayer of Elijah, God did not send rain upon the earth, for how long?

291. Who was the woman who swore that she would kill Elijah because he had destroyed the prophets of Baal?

292. Who organised the building of the first temple at Jerusalem?

293. What was the name of John the Baptist's father?

294. What was the name of his mother?

295. Who was given the promise by God, that he should not die until he had seen the baby Jesus?

296. Who baptized Jesus?

285. *Zebedee. Matt. 4.21.*

286. *The epistle to the Hebrews. Heb. 7.1-4.*

287. *'. . . than for a rich man to enter into the kingdom of God.' Luke 18.25.*

288. *'. . . take heed lest he fall.' 1 Cor. 10.12.*

289. *The Galatians. Gal. 3.1.*

290. *Three years and six months. Jas. 5.17.*

291. *Jezebel. 1 Kings 19.2.*

292. *Solomon. 1 Kings 5.2-5.*

293. *Zacharias. Luke 1.59-63.*

294. *Elisabeth. Luke 1.57.*

295. *Simeon. Luke 2.25-26.*

296. *John the Baptist. Matt. 3.13.*

297. When Jesus was baptized, the Holy Spirit descended upon him in a bodily shape, what was it?

298. In Jesus' parable, how many foolish virgins were there?

299. After the death of Moses, Joshua was told by God to continue in Moses' place. What was the last obstacle in their way before they could enter into the promised land?

300. The river was in flood at this time, so how did they all cross over?

301. Rahab, the harlot is mentioned more than once in the New Testament, because of her faith. What action did she take to aid the children of Israel in their capture of Jericho?

302. What did God tell Joshua to do, so that the crossing of the river Jordan would be remembered by future generations?

303. Gideon asked God to prove to him that he would help the Israelites in their fight against the Midianites and the Amalekites. How did he ask God to do this?

304. What don't men put a lighted candle under?

305. What is the light of the body?

306. Why can't a man serve two masters?

307. Complete the following text: 'The fear of the Lord is the beginning of knowledge . . .'

297. *A dove. Luke 3.22.*

298. *Five. Matt. 25.2.*

299. *The river Jordan. Josh. 1.2.*

300. *God caused the water to stop flowing. Josh. 3.13.*

301. *She hid the two spies which had been sent from Israel's camp. Josh. 2.*

302. *Take twelve stones from the dry river bed, and make them into a pile on the bank. Josh. 4.1-8.*

303. *Gideon would place a sheep's fleece on the ground on two consecutive evenings. The first morning the fleece had to be wet with dew and the ground dry, the second morning the fleece had to be dry and the ground wet. Judg. 6.37-40.*

304. *A bushel. Some translations say a basket, or a bowl. Matt. 5.15.*

305. *The eye. Matt. 6.22.*

306. *'He will either hate one and love the other, or he will hold to one and despise the other.' Matt. 6.24.*

307. *'. . . but fools despise wisdom and instruction.' Prov. 1.7.*

308. Whom did Jesus ask for a drink of water?

309. There are many women called Mary in the New Testament. Which one of them was it out of whom Jesus cast seven devils?

310. When Jesus asked his disciples who they thought he was, which one answered: 'Thou art the Christ'?

311. After Peter had cut off the right ear of the high priest's servant, Jesus rebuked him, telling him that he could pray to God for assistance if he wanted. How many angels did Jesus say that his Father would send him?

312. What was the name of the high priest at the time of Jesus' crucifixion?

313. How old was Noah when he went into the ark?

314. How long did it rain?

315. Who gave the names to every living creature?

316. Jesus cured a blind man in Bethsaida by anointing the man's eyes with spittle, but the remedy required a second application. What did the man reply when Jesus asked him if he could see after the first application?

317. There was an occasion when Jesus was confronted with a devil-possessed man, and he cast the devils out into a herd of animals. What animals were they?

308. *A woman of Samaria. John 4.7.*

309. *Mary Magdalene. Luke 8.2.*

310. *Peter. Mark 8.29.*

311. *More than twelve legions. Matt. 26.53.*

312. *Caiaphas. Matt. 26.57.*

313. *Six hundred years old. Gen. 7.6.*

314. *Forty days and forty nights. Gen. 7.12.*

315. *Adam. Gen. 2.19-20.*

316. *'I see men as trees, walking.' Mark 8.24.*

317. *Swine. Mark 5.13.*

318. In which country did this miracle take place?

319. Why can't a hypocrite pull the mote (or splinter) out of his brother's eye?

320. How are the false prophets said to present themselves so that they can separate the flock?

321. Why are the heathen said to pray with vain repetitions?

322. What are we told to seek, before food, drink and clothing?

323. What happened to the house that was built upon the rock when the rain came and the winds blew?

324. While Paul and Silas were at Philippi, staying at the house of Lydia, they were met by a girl who was possessed by a spirit which Paul cast out, but they were disliked by certain other men because of their action. Why?

325. How were Paul and Silas treated because of their action of casting out the spirit from the girl?

326. What was the inscription upon an altar, that Paul quoted to the Athenians?

327. At which well known landmark was Paul when he preached to the Athenians?

318. *The country of the Gadarenes. Mark 5.1.*

319. *Because he has got a beam (a log) in his own. Matt. 7.4.*

320. *In sheep's clothing. Matt. 7.15.*

321. *Because they think that they shall be heard for their much speaking. Matt. 6.7.*

322. *The kingdom of God, and His righteousness. Matt. 6.33.*

323. *It did not fall. Matt 7.24-25.*

324. *Because the girl was possessed by a 'spirit of divination', and brought her masters much gain by soothsaying. Acts 16.16.*

325. *They were stripped, beaten, and cast into prison. Acts 16.22-23.*

326. *'To the unknown God.' Acts 17.23.*

327. *Mars' hill. Acts 17.22.*

328. God wanted to show Israel that he was helping them in their battles, so he needed to reduce Israel's soldiers to such a degree that the odds against them seemed impossible. How did he tell Gideon to reduce their numbers?

329. How many men did Gideon start off with?

330. How many remained to fight after he had thinned them out?

331. Who vowed a vow that if God would help him win a battle against the Ammonites, he would offer for a burnt offering the first thing that he met coming from his house on his return?

332. What was the first thing that he met on returning home?

333. Did he keep his vow?

334. Who killed a lion with his bare hands?

335. What was the riddle that Samson put to the Philistines?

336. In one of Jesus' parables we are told of a rich man and a beggar, the beggar desiring that he should be fed with the crumbs which fell from the rich man's table. What was the beggar's name?

337. How often was the feast of the passover kept by the Jews?

338. Why was the feast of the passover kept?

328. *All the men who were frightened were told to go home; then when the rest were drinking, all the men who knelt down and sucked the water into their mouth were also sent home. Judg. 7.2-6.*

329. *Thirty-two thousand. Judg. 7.3.*

330. *Three hundred. Judg. 7.8.*

331. *Jephthah. Judg. 11.30-31.*

332. *His only daughter. Judg. 11.32-34.*

333. *Yes. Judg. 11.39.*

334. *Samson. Judg. 14.5-6.*

335. *'Out of the eater came forth meat, and out of the strong came forth sweetness.' Judg. 14.14.*

336. *Lazarus. Luke 16.20.*

337. *Once a year. Exod. 13.9-10.*

338. *To remind them how the angel of death passed over them in Egypt. Exod. 12.13-14.*

339. Jesus remarked about a certain widow who cast some money into the temple treasury; how much did she cast in?

340. When Jacob was blessing Joseph's sons, what did he do that was out of the ordinary which displeased Joseph, who tried to correct his father?

341. Who is said to have written the majority of the book of Psalms?

342. Who was Absalom's father?

343. Just before Jesus was betrayed by Judas, he went with the disciples to a place named Gethsemane, where he left them and went alone to pray. Which three disciples did he separate from the others and tell them to watch?

344. Who came to Jesus and asked him to grant that her two sons should sit, one on his right hand and the other on his left, in his kingdom?

345. How did the request affect the other ten disciples?

346. On what kind of animal did Jesus ride into Jerusalem, as the prophet had foretold that he would?

347. Paul and Silas were held fast in stocks in an inner prison; how were they freed?

348. What time did it happen?

339. *Two mites (small coins). Luke 21.2.*

340. *He blessed the youngest first, instead of the eldest. Gen. 48.17.*

341. *David.*

342. *David. 2 Sam. 19.4.*

343. *Peter, James and John. Mark 14.33.*

344. *The mother of James and John. Matt. 20.21.*

345. *They were indignant at James and John. Matt. 20.24.*

346. *An ass. Matt. 21.7.*

347. *A great earthquake came and all the doors were opened, and everyone's bands were loosed. Acts 16.26.*

348. *Midnight. Acts 16.25.*

349. What were Paul and Silas doing at the time?

350. What did the keeper of the prison do when he awoke and found all the prison doors open?

351. Who was the wife of Aquila?

352. What was Paul's trade and occupation?

353. When Paul left Corinth with Aquila and Priscilla they set sail for where?

354. Why had Paul shaved his head?

355. Who said: 'Remember now thy Creator in the days of thy youth, while the evil days come not, nor the years draw nigh, when thou shalt say, I have no pleasure in them.'?

356. Who found Moses in the bulrushes and raised him as her own child?

357. Who wrote the Old Testament book of Lamentations?

358. Complete the following text: 'For God so loved the world, that he gave his only begotten Son . . .'

359. With whom did Jacob wrestle all night until daybreak?

360. Jacob would not let the man go until he had received something; what was it?

361. What did the man do to free himself from Jacob's grip?

349. *Praying and singing praises to God. Acts 16.25.*

350. *He drew out his sword to kill himself. Acts 16.27.*

351. *Priscilla. Acts 18.2.*

352. *A tentmaker. Acts 18.3.*

353. *Syria. Acts 18.18.*

354. *He had a vow. Acts 18.18.*

355. *King Solomon. Eccles. 12.1.*

356. *Pharaoh's daughter. Exod. 2.5-10.*

357. *Jeremiah.*

358. *'. . . that whosoever believeth in him should not perish, but have everlasting life.' John 3.16.*

359. *A man. Gen. 32.24. Elsewhere called an angel. Hos. 12.4.*

360. *A blessing. Gen. 32.26.*

361. *Touched the hollow of Jacob's thigh and put it out of joint. Gen. 32.25.*

362. What name did Jacob give to the place afterwards?

363. Why did Pharaoh order that all the male Hebrew children should be killed?

364. How long was Moses on mount Sinai receiving the commandments?

365. Methuselah lived for 969 years, and is the oldest man on record. Who was the second oldest?

366. How old was Noah when he died?

367. According to the book of Revelation how many plagues are to be sent upon the earth before the end of time?

368. Only three of the original disciples have left a written record or epistle in the New Testament. Who are they?

369. Who was trapped when the mule that he was riding on ran under an oak tree, and his head became entangled in the lower branches?

370. Who killed Absalom with three darts while he was still trapped?

371. After Jesus had fasted for forty days and forty nights in the wilderness, he was tempted by the devil. What, according to Matthew's Gospel, was the first temptation?

372. What was the second temptation?

362.	*Peniel. Gen. 32.30.*

363.	*Their numbers were so great it was feared that, in the event of war, they would join with Egypt's enemies. Exod. 1.8-10.*

364.	*Forty days and forty nights. Exod. 24.18.*

365.	*Jared. Gen. 5.20.*

366.	*Nine hundred and fifty years. Gen. 9.29.*

367.	*Seven. Rev. 15.1.*

368.	*Matthew, John, Peter.*

369.	*Absalom. 2 Sam. 18.9.*

370.	*Joab. 2 Sam. 18.14.*

371.	*To turn stones into bread. Matt. 4.3.*

372.	*To cast himself off a pinnacle of the temple and let the angels catch him. Matt. 4.6.*

373. What was the third temptation?

374. What was the name of the king who caused Daniel to be thrown into the den of lions?

375. Did the king want to do it?

376. Then why did he have to do it?

377. Why was Lot's wife turned into a pillar of salt?

378. When the angel stopped Abraham from offering Isaac as a sacrifice, what did he use instead?

379. Where did the ram come from?

380. How many brothers did Goliath have?

381. What did they all have in common?

382. One of them is reported to have had some very odd characteristics besides being a giant; what were they?

383. In what town were they born?

384. Which two disciples did Jesus send to prepare the room for the passover?

385. To whom did God make the promise: 'I will make thy seed as the dust of the earth: so that if a man can number the dust of the earth, then shall thy seed also be numbered.'?

386. On which day did the Holy Spirit fill the disciples?

373. *To fall down and worship Satan in repayment for all of the kingdoms of the world, and the glory of them. Matt. 4.8-9.*

374. *Darius. Dan. 6.1.*

375. *No. Dan. 6.14.*

376. *Once a decree had been made according to the law of the Medes and Persians, it could not be altered. Dan. 6.12.*

377. *Because she looked back towards Sodom. Gen. 19.26.*

378. *A ram. Gen. 22.13.*

379. *It was caught in a thicket by its horns. Gen. 22.13.*

380. *Four. 2 Sam. 21.15-22.*

381. *They were all giants. 2 Sam. 21.15-22.*

382. *He had six fingers on each hand and six toes on each foot. 2 Sam. 21.20.*

383. *Gath. 2 Sam. 21.15-22.*

384. *Peter and John. Luke 22.8.*

385. *Abram. Gen. 13.16.*

386. *The day of Pentecost. Acts 2.1-4.*

387. In what form was the Holy Spirit seen?

388. When the people of Jerusalem heard the disciples speaking in other tongues, what did they say was wrong with them?

389. It was when Jacob wrestled with the man at Peniel that he was first called by a new name; what was it?

390. What was the name of Joseph's wife?

391. What was the name of the young man who fell asleep while Paul was preaching, and fell out of the third storey window?

392. How many men did the twelve disciples appoint to be separated to the particular work of looking after the widows in the daily ministration?

393. How many daughters did Philip the evangelist have?

394. What was their particular gift?

395. How did king Saul die?

396. When king Saul was dead, the Philistines cut off his head; what did they do with it?

397. What did they do with the remainder of his body?

398. What was the name of the woman with whom David committed adultery?

387. *Like cloven tongues of fire. Acts 2.3.*

388. *They said that they were drunk. Acts 2.13.*

389. *Israel. Gen. 32.28.*

390. *Asenath. Gen. 41.45.*

391. *Eutychus. Acts 20.9.*

392. *Seven. Acts 6.1-3.*

393. *Four. Acts 21.8-9.*

394. *Prophecy. Acts 21.8-9.*

395. *He committed suicide. 1 Sam. 31.4.*

396. *They sent it around all the land to show everybody. 1 Sam. 31.9.*

397. *Fastened it to the wall of Beth-shan. 1 Sam. 31.10.*

398. *Bathsheba. 2 Sam. 11.3-5.*

399. Who was Bathsheba's husband?

400. How did David get rid of Uriah so that he could marry his wife?

401. What was the name of the prophet whom God sent to David to rebuke him for what he had done?

402. What punishment did Nathan prophesy to David, because of what he had done?

403. How long did David lie upon the ground and fast, beseeching God to save the child?

404. What was the name of the next son that David and Bathsheba had?

405. What is the fourth book of the Old Testament?

406. What is the tenth commandment?

407. What was the name of the prophet who took Paul's girdle, bound his own hands and feet with it, and prophesied that the man to whom the girdle belonged should be bound in a like manner and handed over to the Gentiles?

408. Where did the prophet come from?

409. When did the prophecy come true?

410. Who then accused Paul to the Romans?

411. What did the chief captain of the Romans order to be done to Paul?

399. *Uriah the Hittite. 2 Sam. 11.3.*

400. *He ordered him into the hottest part of the battle, where he died. 2 Sam. 11.15-17.*

401. *Nathan. 2 Sam. 12.1.*

402. *The child would die. 2 Sam. 12.14.*

403. *Seven days. 2 Sam. 12.18.*

404. *Solomon. 2 Sam. 12.24.*

405. *Numbers.*

406. *Thou shalt not covet. Exod. 20.17.*

407. *Agabus. Acts 21.10-11.*

408. *Judaea. Acts 21.10*

409. *A short while after, when Paul was in Jerusalem. Acts 21.30-33.*

410. *The Jews. Acts 22.30.*

411. *That he should be examined by scourging. Acts 22.24.*

412. When they were tying Paul up ready to be whipped, he told one of the soldiers something which brought fear upon them all. What was it?

413. Why did this news make them all so frightened?

414. What kind of a plant did Jonah sit under while he waited to see what would happen to Ninevah?

415. What was the tree that the serpent tempted Eve to eat of?

416. After both Adam and Eve had eaten of the tree of knowledge of good and evil, they were driven from the garden lest they should eat of another tree, what was it?

417. How was the garden of Eden then protected so that they could not return and eat of the tree of life?

418. Complete the following text: 'To everything there is a season . . .'

419. Who, are we told, is the 'author and finisher of our faith'?

420. Who was it that collected all the gold together and made the molten calf for the Israelites to worship?

421. Where did the gold come from?

412.   *That he, too, was a Roman. Acts 22.25.*

413.   *It was against the law to whip a Roman unless he had been condemned by the correct authority. It would seem that it was also against Roman law that a Roman should even be bound. Acts 22.25-29.*

414.   *A gourd. Jonah 4.6.*

415.   *The tree of knowledge of good and evil. Gen. 2.9.*

416.   *The tree of life. Gen. 3.22.*

417.   *Cherubims and a flaming sword barred the way. Gen. 3.24.*

418.   *'. . . and a time to every purpose under the heaven.' Eccles. 3.1.*

419.   *Jesus. Heb. 12.2.*

420.   *Aaron. Exod. 32.3-4.*

421.   *From the Israelite's golden earrings. Exod. 32.2.*

422. There were two malefactors crucified alongside Jesus, and one of them asked a request of Jesus. What was it?

423. How did Jesus reply?

424. What was the name of the angel that appeared to Zacharias, and foretold the birth of John the Baptist?

425. Zacharias asked the angel for a sign to show him that God would do as the angel had said. Why did he doubt?

426. What was the sign that God gave him?

427. Eight days after the child was born he was to be circumcized; what name did the priests call him?

428. Who told them that his name was going to be John?

429. How did Zacharias confirm this, as he still could not speak?

430. What happened as soon as Zacharias had written down that the child should be called John?

431. While Paul was still being held in the Roman castle at Jerusalem, some of the Jews bound themselves under a curse; what was it?

432. How many Jews were involved in the conspiracy curse?

433. Who told Paul about the plot?

422. *'Remember me when thou comest into thy kingdom.' Luke 23.42.*

423. *'Verily I say unto thee, Today shalt thou be with me in paradise.' Luke 23.43.*

424. *Gabriel. Luke 1.19.*

425. *Because both he and his wife were very old. Luke 1.18.*

426. *He was struck dumb until the child was born. Luke 1.20.*

427. *Zacharias, after the name of his father. Luke 1.59.*

428. *The child's mother. Luke 1.60.*

429. *He wrote it down. Luke 1.63.*

430. *His tongue was loosed, and he spoke, and praised God. Luke 1.64.*

431. *That they would neither eat nor drink until they had killed Paul. Acts 23.12-13.*

432. *More than forty. Acts 23.12-13.*

433. *His sister's son. Acts 23.16.*

434. How many soldiers did the Roman chief captain order to guard Paul as they moved him to the castle of Felix?

435. What position of authority did Felix hold?

436. Who was Felix's wife?

437. What nationality was she?

438. Complete the following text: 'Blessed are the merciful . . .'

439. According to Matthew's Gospel, how many brothers did Jesus have?

440. What was the final plague that God sent upon Egypt, that caused Pharaoh to let the Hebrews go?

441. How were the Hebrews to mark their houses, so that the angel of death would pass over them?

442. How were the Egyptians stopped from following the Israelites through the sea until the time was right?

443. On the front of Aaron's mitre there was a golden plate with an inscription on it. What was the inscription?

444. When Cain was driven out from the presence of God because he had killed Abel, where did he go to live?

434. *200 soldiers, 70 horsemen, and 200 spearmen. Acts 23.23.*

435. *Roman Governor. Acts 23.24.*

436. *Drusilla. Acts 24.24.*

437. *A Jewess. Acts 24.24.*

438. *'. . . for they shall obtain mercy.' Matt. 5.7.*

439. *Four. Matt. 13.55.*

440. *The killing of all of Egypt's firstborn. Exod. 12.29.*

441. *They had to mark the door posts of their houses with blood. Exod. 12.7.*

442. *They were covered by a cloud of darkness and could not see. Exod. 14.19, 20.*

443. *HOLINESS TO THE LORD. Exod. 28.36-37.*

444. *The land of Nod. Gen. 4.16.*

445. Which was the first bird that Noah sent out from the ark to see if the water had abated?

446. Which bird came back with an olive leaf?

447. Rachel died during the birth of one of Jacob's sons; which one was it?

448. In Acts we are told of a Jew from Alexandria, an eloquent man and well learned in the scriptures. What was his name?

449. Who 'expounded to him the way of God more perfectly'?

450. Paul stayed in Ephesus for how many years?

451. Of his time in Ephesus, Paul spent the first three months teaching in the synagogue, but when the Jews turned against him he taught in a school; whose school was it?

452. God worked special miracles by the hand of Paul while he was in Ephesus; how were they put into effect?

453. How many sons did Sceva have?

454. What were Sceva's sons looked upon as being?

455. On one occasion Sceva's sons tried to exorcise an evil spirit from a man with the words: 'We adjure you by Jesus whom Paul preacheth . . .' What reply did the evil spirit give?

456. What happened next?

445. *A raven. Gen. 8.7.*

446. *A dove. Gen. 8.11.*

447. *Benjamin. Gen. 35.18.*

448. *Apollos. Acts 18.24-28.*

449. *Aquila and Priscilla. Acts 18.26.*

450. *Two. Acts 19.10.*

451. *The school of Tyrannus. Acts 19.9.*

452. *His handkerchiefs or aprons were taken to the sick, and they recovered. Acts 19.11-12.*

453. *Seven. Acts 19.14.*

454. *Vagabond Jews, exorcists. Acts 19.13.*

455. *'Jesus I know, and Paul I know; but who are ye?' Acts 19.15.*

456. *The man leapt upon them and overcame them so that they fled, naked and wounded. Acts 19.16.*

457. Many people in Ephesus who used 'curious arts' brought their books out and burned them before the rest of the city. What was the value of all the books burned?

458. What was the name of the silversmith who made shrines to the goddess Diana for a living, and stirred up the people when he saw that Paul's doctrine was going to put him out of business?

459. What new name did Jesus give to Simon, brother of Andrew?

460. What does Cephas mean?

461. Jesus said that men do not put new wine into old bottles. Why?

462. Paul commended a woman who lived at Cenchrea, in his letter to the Romans, saying 'she hath been a succourer of many, and of myself also.' Who was she?

463. In his letter to the Romans, Paul says: 'We then that are strong ought to . . .' What is it that we ought to do?

464. Which one of the disciples did Jesus rebuke with the words: 'Get thee behind me, Satan: thou art an offence unto me.'?

465. Why did Jesus speak to Peter in this way?

466. Cain and Abel both brought offerings to God; what did Cain bring?

467. What did Abel bring?

457. *Fifty thousand pieces of silver. Acts 19.19.*

458. *Demetrius. Acts 19.24.*

459. *Cephas. John 1.42.*

460. *A stone. John 1.42.*

461. *'. . . else the bottles break, and the wine
runneth out, and the bottles perish.'
Matt. 9.17.*

462. *Phoebe. Rom. 16.1.*

463. *'. . . bear the infirmities of the weak.'
Rom. 15.1.*

464. *Peter. Matt. 16.23.*

465. *Because Peter tried to dissuade Jesus from
going to Jerusalem to die. Matt. 16.22.*

466. *The fruit of the ground. Gen. 4.3.*

467. *The first born of his flock. Gen. 4.4.*

468. Which one of the two did God accept?

469. What affect did this have on Cain?

470. What relation was Absalom to Amnon?

471. What did King Herod ask the wise men to do when they found the baby Jesus?

472. Why didn't they do as they were asked?

473. With whom did Paul tell Timothy he had left his cloak?

474. Who was Timothy's mother?

475. There was an occasion when certain men asked for tribute money from Peter and Jesus; where did Jesus tell Peter to get it from?

476. Who were Moses' mother and father?

477. When the Pharisees were questioning John the Baptist about who he was, he told them that there was one coming after him who was preferred before him. What article of Jesus' attire did he say he was not worthy to unloose?

478. On one occasion when Jesus was disputing with the Pharisees, he told them that if they destroyed the temple he would raise it up again. How many days did he say it would be accomplished in?

479. To what was Jesus actually referring?

468. *Abel's. Gen. 4.4.*

469. *It made him angry, so that he killed Abel. Gen. 4.5-8.*

470. *They were brothers. 2 Sam. 13.1.*

471. *To return and tell him where the child was. Matt. 2.8.*

472. *They were warned in a dream by God. Matt. 2.12.*

473. *Carpus. 2 Tim. 4.13.*

474. *Eunice. 2 Tim. 1.5.*

475. *Out of a fish's mouth. Matt. 17.27.*

476. *Amram and Jochebed. Exod. 6.20.*

477. *His shoe's latchet, or sandal thong. John 1.27.*

478. *Three days. John 2.19.*

479. *His own body. John 2.21.*

480. Complete the following text: 'Behold, I send you forth as sheep in the midst of wolves . . .'

481. When Joseph's brothers went back to their father to fetch Benjamin, Joseph commanded that one of them should remain as his hostage. Which one remained?

482. When Paul was in Ephesus there was an occasion when the theatre was filled with people who cried out the same thing over and over again; what was it?

483. For how long did they cry out these words?

484. Of which trade and occupation was Joseph, Jesus' father?

485. In the parable of the talents the first man received ten, the second man received five, the third man only one. What did the man who received one do with it?

486. Name Jesus' four brothers, as mentioned in Matthew's Gospel.

487. During Jesus' travels he entered into Peter's house with some of the disciples, but one of Peter's relatives was sick and was cured by Jesus; who was it?

488. How many times did Moses get married?

489. His second wife was not a Hebrew; what country was she from?

480. '. . . be ye therefore wise as serpents, and harmless as doves.' Matt. 10.16.

481. Simeon. Gen. 42.24.

482. 'Great is Diana of the Ephesians.' Acts 19.34.

483. Two hours. Acts 19.34.

484. A carpenter. Matt. 13.55.

485. He dug in the ground and hid it. Matt. 25.18.

486. James, Joses, Simon, Judas. Matt. 13.55.

487. His wife's mother. Mark 1.30-31.

488. Twice.

489. Ethiopia. Num. 12.1.

490. Complete the following text: 'Blessed are the poor in spirit . . .'

491. While Paul was being held by Festus, to whom did he appeal?

492. Why did he take this action?

493. While Paul was travelling to Rome, the ship that he was aboard was caught in a storm; how long did it last?

494. How many people were on board the ship?

495. Upon which island did they eventually land?

496. When they were making fires to dry themselves out, Paul picked up some wood and something crawled out of the pile and bit him. What was it?

497. What did the natives say when they saw this, knowing that he was a prisoner?

498. When Paul didn't drop down dead as the natives expected, what did they think he was?

499. Of the ten lepers that Jesus cured only one came back to thank him; what city was he from?

500. Complete the following text: 'Foxes have holes, and birds of the air have nests . . .'

490. *'. . . for theirs is the kingdom of heaven.'*
Matt. 5.3.

491. *Caesar. Acts 25.11.*

492. *Because he was a Roman citizen.*
Festus had asked him to go back to Jerusalem
to be judged by the Jews. Acts 25.9.

493. *Fourteen days. Acts 27.27.*

494. *Two hundred and seventy-six. Acts 27.37.*

495. *Melita (Malta) Acts 28.1.*

496. *A viper. Acts 28.3.*

497. *They said that he was no doubt a murderer,*
and he was getting what he deserved. Acts
28.4.

498. *A god. Acts 28.6.*

499. *Samaria. Luke 17.16-18.*

500. *'. . . but the Son of man hath not where to lay*
his head.' Luke 9.58.